CELEBRATING THE PEOPLES AND CIVILIZATIONS OF AFRICA™

THE
ASANTE
OF WEST AFRICA

Jamie Hetfield

The Rosen Publishing Group's
PowerKids Press™
New York

Published in 1996 by The Rosen Publishing Group, Inc.
29 East 21st Street, New York, NY 10010

First Edition

Book design: Kim Sonsky

Photo credits: Cover and pp. 4, 7, 8, 11, 16, 19, 20 © Jeffrey Jay Foxx; pp. 12, 15 © Herbert M. Cole.

Hetfield, Jamie.
    The Asante of West Africa / Jamie Hetfield.
        p.   cm. — (Celebrating the peoples and civilizations of Africa)
    Includes index.
    Summary: Briefly describes the beliefs, traditions, food, clothes, and gold jewelry of the Ashante of Ghana.
    ISBN 0-8239-2329-0
    1. Ashanti (African people)—History—Juvenile literature. 2. Ashanti (African people)—Social life and customs—Juvenile literature. [1. Ashanti (African people)] I. Title. II. Series.
DT507.H47 1996
966'.004963385—dc20
                                                  96-10652
                                                         CIP
                                                         AC

Manufactured in the United States of America

CONTENTS

WHO ARE THE ASANTE?

The **Asante** (uh-SHON-tay) are one of many peoples in Africa. They are famous all over the world for making beautiful gold jewelry and weaving fine cloth. The Asante are very proud of their history and their heritage. Nearly two hundred years ago, the Asante Kingdom was one of the richest, most powerful kingdoms in Africa.

◀ The Asante have a long and proud history.

5

WHERE DO THE ASANTE LIVE?

Most Asante live on the west coast of Africa in a country called Ghana. Ghana is about the same size as the state of Oregon. Its capital is Accra. About 75 different peoples live there. Ghana was once called the Gold Coast because there is so much gold there.

Many Asante live in modern cities. Some Asante towns and villages are found in the beautiful green rain forests. In the rain forests of West Africa, there are so many trees and branches that you can barely see the sky!

Many Asante live in cities, such as Kumasi. ▶

TOWNS AND VILLAGES

Some Asante live in small villages in the rain forest. To get from village to village, they walk along narrow footpaths through the forest. Bigger towns and cities have buses, trucks, taxis, and roads.

In the forest many houses are small and rectangular. The walls are made of wood and clay. The roofs are made from leaves.

Inside, sleeping mats cover part of the ground. Fireplaces are painted with a bright red clay. Beautiful pottery lamps light the insides of the houses at night.

◀ Paths through the beautiful forest often lead from one village to the next.

ASANTE MEALS

Asante men once hunted animals in the rain forest. They ate the meat of wild pigs, antelopes, elephants, and other animals. Now the Asante buy meat because there aren't as many animals around. Asante women and children still catch freshwater crabs and fish from rivers. Giant forest snails make a tasty stew.

The Asante are also farmers. They grow many crops, such as corn, **cassava** (kuh-SAH-vuh), oranges, tomatoes, **plantains** (PLAN-tenz), peppers, and peanuts.

Corn is just one of the many crops that Asante farmers grow. ▶

KENTE CLOTH

The Asante are famous for weaving **kente** (KEN-tay) cloth. The strong colors and pretty patterns of kente cloth have special meanings. For example, yellow stands for the yolk of an egg. Blue means the sky.

Kente cloth was once woven of silk thread and worn only by the Asante royal family. Today, cotton kente cloth is made in many places in the world and can be worn by everyone.

◄ The Asante continue to weave beautiful kente cloth by traditional methods.

GOLD

In the days of the Asante Kingdom, traders used to weigh their gold on special scales. Beautiful little gold figures were used as **weights** (WAYTS). Some of these figures of animals or people had special meanings. They reminded the Asante of important stories or sayings. Today, these gold weights can be seen in museums.

Now the Asante use paper money and coins for trade. They still make beautiful gold jewelry in the shapes of bells, stools, musical instruments, weapons, and snakes.

The Asante are famous for their work with gold. ▶

FAMILY AND COMMUNITY

The Asante trace their family roots through their mothers. In many Asante villages, all of the villagers are related to the same female **ancestor** (AN-ses-ter). The head of the village is the eldest male relative of that ancestor.

In the United States, a person's most important male relative is often his or her father. For an Asante, the most important person is his or her mother's brother. In fact, Asante boys often live with those uncles. When an Asante man dies, his wealth goes to his sister's sons, not his own sons.

◀ Women play an important role in Asante society.

17

THE IMPORTANCE OF BEING CLEAN

The Asante believe that dirt carries danger and disease. Being clean is important. Asante leaders always wear shoes. If their feet touch dirt, the Asante believe, bad things will happen to the village.

The Asante have a special sweeping **ceremony** (SAYR-uh-mone-ee) to clean a village of danger and disease. The women and children walk from one end of the village to the other, singing prayers. As they walk, they pretend to sweep the street with the brooms they carry.

The Asante have many old rituals and customs they follow even today. ▶

THE GOLDEN STOOL

Most Asante have their own stools. These wooden chairs are shaped like little benches with the ends turned up. They are decorated with beautiful carvings. The Asante believe a person's spirit is connected to his stool. No one sits on these stools.

The Golden Stool is the throne of a great Asante king who lived almost two hundred years ago. It is covered in gold. It is believed that whoever owns this stool is the true ruler of the Asante. The Golden Stool is passed down to the oldest son of the ruler's sister.

◀ Because of their importance in Asante society, stools are carved with great care.

THE ASANTE TODAY

Today, some Asante live in big modern cities and have jobs like the ones your parents have. Their children go to school like you. But many Asante continue to farm and live in villages in the rain forest.

The Asante Kingdom is now part of Ghana. The Asante are very proud of their **traditions** (tra-DISH-unz). Many Asante still see the king as their leader. They still believe in the power of the Golden Stool.

GLOSSARY

ancestor (AN-ses-ter) Relative who lived before
you.

Asante (uh-SHON-tay) A people who live in
western Africa.

cassava (kuh-SAH-vuh) Vegetable that is somewhat
like a potato.

ceremony (SAYR-uh-mone-ee) Formal act or set of
acts that have a special meaning.

kente (KEN-tay) Asante cloth whose colors and
patterns have special meanings.

plantain (PLAN-ten) Starchy fruit; similar to a
banana.

tradition (tra-DISH-un) The way a group of people
has done things for many years.

weight (WAYT) Piece of metal, like gold, whose
exact weight is known.

23

INDEX

24

DATE DUE

MAR 2 6 '98			
FEB 2 8 '00			
-DEC 03 2016 iu#168225893 PPM			